ADLESTROPHES
OR
THE POETS MAKE AN EXCURSION TO ADLESTROP

ADLESTROPHES

OR

THE POETS MAKE AN EXCURSION TO ADLESTROP

by

R. K. R. Thornton

καὶ μικρὸν προελθὼν Δαμάστην ἐν Ἐρινεῷ τὸν Προκρούστην, ἀναγκάσας
αὐτὸν ἀπισοῦν τοῖς κλιντῆρσιν ὥσπερ τοὺς ξένους ἐκεῖνος.
Plutarch, Life of Theseus, XI

R. K. R. THORNTON at the RECTORY PRESS

2014

To be had from R. K. R. Thornton at the
Rectory Press,
2 Rectory Terrace,
Gosforth,
Newcastle upon Tyne NE3 1XY
England

rkrthornton@btinternet.com

Fourth (augmented) edition limited to 100 copies

ISBN 978-0-9572415-0-3

Typeset in Palatino and printed in England on recycled paper by
Imprintdigital

INTRODUCTION

This book is an expansion and re-ordering of my earlier series of versions of Edward Thomas's poem, written to explore how other poets might have addressed Thomas's material. I blamed it on Anne Harvey, who gave me a copy of her anthology Adlestrop Revisited *(Sutton Publishing 1999 and 2000, and reprinted 2009 and 2011 by the History Press). Unpromising as a book on one sixteen-line poem might seem, it is a fascinating read – at least to those who, like me, can find enjoyment in seeing a souvenir programme that dates his journey, the railway timetable which shows that he probably wasn't on an express train at all that day, and poems and essays and plays all growing out of Thomas's deceptively slight verses.*

That there are other such people was proved by a book to which Simon Court introduced me – Leonard McDermid's And for that Minute, *privately printed at his Stichill Marigold Press by the author in 2009. He imagines statements (modelled on Thomas's poem) from witnesses of the unscheduled halt – the engineman, the passenger guard, the lampman, the general carrier, a casual farm servant, and the signalman, and juxtaposes them with railway regulations from 1904. It's worth looking out.*

I don't know what started me making other versions of the poem as if by a variety of authors. Perhaps at the end of reading the book, everything seemed to smack of Adlestrop. Perhaps it was my dissatisfaction with some of the offerings of other poets writing on the theme of 'Adlestrop' but never quite getting near it. And having done one small booklet, I was encouraged to make it larger.

I did contemplate concocting a more elaborate shape, making a sort of Canterbury Tales *compilation of pilgrims to*

Adlestrop, or perhaps a short story of the authors gathering to make the train journey; and I amused myself for a time in inventing their conversation on the way, with its mixture of medieval brusqueness, eighteenth-century politeness, Jesuitical precision. nineteenth-century roguery, and Decadent languor. But in the end it seemed that the verses were what I was interested in, and so l let it go at that. You can invent the trip for yourselves.

Three things to note. First, that some of the incidental details from Anne Harvey's book found their way into the poems, although they were not in Thomas's original – like the notebooks, and the exact date. Second, that the versions are in no way aiming to diminish Thomas's splendid poem. In fact the writing of them has taught me just how tough and well-constructed his poem is, and how difficult to re-invent its magic. Third, that I owe both much encouragement and some lines to Alistair Elliot.

The epigraph, by the way, is meant to look pretentious, to give a sense of scholarly dignity to what might otherwise seem a frivolous exercise, like those quotations which the writers of the eighteenth century would put on their title pages. I can't pretend to be fluent in Greek and so I don't expect you to be, so I offer you this translation: 'and going a little farther, at Erineus, he killed Damastes, surnamed Procrustes, by compelling him to make his own body fit his bed, as he had been wont to do with those of strangers'. *I suppose that should be a dire warning to me.*

And while I'm explaining things, some people have asked me who the individuals are on the cover. On the front cover on the left the red-headed Algernon Charles Swinburne leans forward in front of a languid Ernest Dowson, while behind them the turbaned Alexander Pope faces Gerard Manley Hopkins, who sits quietly in the corner in his soutane. Edward Thomas, with his country man's boots, sits next to Geoffrey Chaucer, who is probably pointing out some ribaldry to Swinburne. On the back cover in the next compartment A. A. Milne tries to ignore the smoking e e cummings, while Robert Frost is taking no notice of the histrionic William McGonagall. McGonagall is nearly treading on the toes of his beloved Shakespeare. In front of Shakespeare Wordsworth retains his calm, while A. E. Housman and Thomas Hardy are keeping themselves to themselves.

KELSEY THORNTON

2012

In reprinting this book for a third hundred copies, I have taken the opportunity to make two small corrections and to add another carriage for Rudyard Kipling, who for some reason missed getting into the carriage with the others. Or did they not allow him in?

September 2012

This fourth edition has some additional passengers, some more pictures, and some further contributors, since friends were amused to try their hands at the game, and I thought they might as well hop on board. The train seems to be getting almost crowded.

January 2014

FOR HILARY

ADLESTROP
the original by
EDWARD THOMAS (1878-1917)

Yes. I remember Adlestrop –
The name, because one afternoon
Of heat the express drew up there
Unwontedly. It was late June.

The steam hissed. Someone cleared his throat.
No one went and no one came
On the bare platform. What I saw
Was Adlestrop – only the name

And willows, willow-herb, and grass,
And meadowsweet, and haycocks dry,
No whit less still and lonely fair
Than the high cloudlets in the sky.

And for that minute a blackbird sang
Close by, and round him, mistier,
Farther and farther all the birds
Of Oxfordshire and Gloucestershire.

A PROSE WRITER

A poet went to Adlestrop station on a hot June day in a train, which made an unscheduled stop there. Someone coughed and the steam train let off steam, but there was nothing to see on the platform, except the name of the station. In the vicinity there were various trees and flowers and evidence of farming, and there were some small clouds that looked like high white bunches of hay. Just then a bird whistled and it seemed as if it set off lots of other birds whistling in the two neighbouring counties.

GEOFFREY CHAUCER (c.1343-1400)

Whan that in June benethe a ful hote sunne
My journey unto Gloster had bigonne,
Bifel that in that seson on a day
Within a train it chaunced that I lay
That strangely made an un-forevisioned stop
Beside a place ycleped Adlestrop.
And though for certeyn I must be to blame
I have al things forgot, except the name.
The steam went from the engine with a hiss,
And sum man coughed, his throte to clear ywis.
Both up and down besemed that al and som
Had left the place and that none else would come.
And ever and anon all that I spyed
Was Adlestrop the name and nought beside
Save willow, meadow sweet and eke the gras
And willowherb that by them growing was.
And wider in the fields I might espye
Haycocks that lay beneath the sun to dry.
The clouds above in rows were clene and white
Like to a harvest in the hevens bright.
See the fresshe flowers how they springe;
Herkneth the blissful briddes how they sing;
For lo the blackbird sang with merye steven
And all the other foules under heven
Unto his carolling made their replye
In misty rings that went both far and high;
From every bough the briddes in accorde,
Sang out through Gloucestershire and Oxenforde.

WILLIAM SHAKESPEARE (1564-1616)

I would not to the running true of trains
Admit impediment. This train drew up
On what, compared with other summer's days,
Was just as lovely but less temperate.
And when you this unexpected halt relate
Speak of it as it was. Nothing extenuate
Nor set down aught in fancy. Then must you speak
Of one who recalls not clearly or too well
The hissing steam and clearing of the throat,
And, looking round, perplexed in the extreme
That all that could be seen was 'Adlestrop',
The signpost at the station; of one who scanned
The willows, willow herb and meadowsweet
And haycocks dry and in whose upturned eyes
Dazzled tears rose from meadows next the sun.
Set down this: say once, in Adlestrop,
When an unscheduled and unpeopled train
Stopped, and a blackbird from a bush close by
Threw all the birds of Gloucester in a state,
And spread contagion into Oxfordshire,
I took from my pouch my little book of notes
And wrote it, thus.

MATSUO BASHŌ (1644-1694)
from the Japanese

Engine's unplanned halt;
In hush of midsummer noon
Ripples of bird song.

ALEXANDER POPE (1688-1744)

What strange emotion up from nothing springs;
What curious memories rise from trivial things,
I sing, as Adlestrop – the name – will find
A place in the recesses of the mind
Because one day late in the month of June
The train made halt there in the heat of noon;
For though the schedule ruled out Adlestrop
Fate had decreed that there the train should stop.
Release of steam issued a hissing note
And someone somewhere coughed to clear his throat;
But observation with extensive care
Surveyed the platform and still found it bare;
Silence succeeding thus to keep at bay
Potential patrons of the iron way.
With none to leave and none to board the trains,
Nought but the name of Adlestrop remains.
Willows stood still, the grass beneath their feet
Made green the banks, with spots of meadowsweet,
Round fields where haystacks in profusion lay
Smiling at heaven in the summer day,
While white and clear the clouds, divinely fair,
Made a new harvest in the fields of air.
A stillness for that minute held the land
Till far the blackest of the feathered band
Sang in the hedgerows that were close at hand.
From out his golden bill he flung a cry;
The walls, the woods, the hedgerows made reply

And other birds and singers took the strain
As widening ripples answered it again,
Filling the whole of Gloucester with its choir
And towered Oxford and its misty shire.

WILLIAM WORDSWORTH (1770-1850)

It stopped amid untraveled ways
Deep in the countryside,
A train that there were none to praise
And very few to ride.

Earth hath not anything to show more bare;
Keen would he be of eye who could discern
A sign that passengers might here return.
The station now doth like a garment wear
The quietness of noon, nor do we care
For hissing steam or cough, nor can we learn
Why the train halted. Everywhere we turn
Only the name of Adlestrop is there.
The sun however beautifully bakes
In splendour lines of haystack, willow, cloud,
A blackbird with a sudden anthem breaks
The calm so deep by whistling aloud.
Dear God, the very counties seem awake
As all their birds rise in a hymning crowd.

ROBERT SOUTHEY (1774-1843)

It was a summer at midday,
    With Edward's trip half done;
The train, which calm and peaceful lay
    Beneath a glaring sun,
Had stopped, but in it could be seen
Some old boy's grandchild Wilhelmine.

She saw her brother Peterkin
    Had something in his hand
Though what it was she couldn't see
    But he seemed to understand
Why the express had made a stop
All unforeseen at Adlestrop,

'What is it that you're holding there?
    That seems it can explain
The reason why we now are in
    A stationary train?'
'Dear sister, this is Bradshaw's book,'
And added kindly 'Have a look'.

'But surely in the schedule there
    It says we would not stop
At some benighted station
    With the name of Adlestrop.'
'I know that to be true,' said he,
'Perhaps it's an emergency.'

'Why? What is happening?' she asked.
    'Just nothing,' he replied.

'The platform is as silent as
    If somebody had died.
And all that one can hear is this:
A man's cough and an engine's hiss.'

But Edward was a country man
    Who knew his birds and flowers
And tried to keep them occupied
    For hours and hours and hours
By pointing to each rural sound
And every flower that grew around.

Willow he named, and willow herb
    And meadowsweet and hay,
And said the clouds were bright and white
    On that midsummer day;
And then from out a nearby bush
A blackbird broke the magic hush.

The sound was joined by all the birds
    In nearby Gloucestershire,
And this was taken up by those
    Also in Oxfordshire.
It did amuse the girls and boys,
But made an awful lot of noise.

But what the train had stopped there for
    To hear the blackbird's shout
And why it hissed and why he coughed
    I never could make out.
But never mind; it could be worse.
It made a subject for a verse.

JOHN KEATS (1795-1821)

ODE TO A BLACKBIRD

My brain aches and a drowsy numbness steals
    Into the train, where I was but a guest,
As though of hemlock it had drunk; the wheels
    Halted and, where it stopped, there did it rest;
The engine lay there, nerveless, listless, dead,
    Like a god still couchant on the iron way,
        Its fires reduced to but a dying ember
          But if I shake my head
    Here upon this trancèd summer day,
        Yes, Adlestrop I think I do remember.

There issued forth one solitary hiss
    Of steam that broke the silence and died off,
Like smoke from dismal fires of darkest Dis;
    Then, answering, one disembodied cough;
No creature on the platform dared to stand,
    And on the other emptiness replied.
        No one was seen to go and no one came
          Though up and down I scanned.
    No soul was evident on either side.
        I noticed only Adelstrop, the name

The melancholy willow and the herb
    That shares its name, and all the summer grass
The scythe has been reluctant to disturb,
    Now in a mournful choir whisper 'alas',

19

They had to admit that the young man looked rather ill

And as Narcissus, glorious to view,
Admires his mirrored image in the glass
  Of the silvery pool where Echo sees him gaze
    And finds she loves him too,
The cloudlets see their image as they pass
  O'er verdurous glooms and winding mossy ways.

Now for that moment do I hear thy strain,
  Gold-billed, swart-wingèd Dryad of the trees,
Transcend the misty silence of the train,
  Singing of summer in full-throated ease.
Thou wast not born for calm, disturbing bird,
  No county limitations pin thee down.
    Thy voice is echoed in the distant mist
      As soon as it is heard
  By birds from Gloucester and from Oxford town,
    That summon us to some imagined tryst.

ALFRED, LORD TENNYSON (1809-92)

On either side the railway stand
The platforms, empty and unmanned,
For stopping there had not been planned
To put down folk on either hand
 In quiet Adlestrop;
And up and down nobody came;
The fields and wolds were just the same;
Nothing to see except the name
 That labelled Adlestrop.

Aspens quiver, willows whiten,
Clouds against the blue sky brighten,
No-one from the train alighting;
Interrupts the poet writing
 Notes on Adlestrop,
Who, gazing from his railway carriage
And sad about his fragile marriage,
Considered no-one would disparage
 Lines on Adlestrop.

Clouds in the blue and perfect weather
Hung like stooks of whitest feather
And one could not determine whether
Hay were cloud or both together
 Hung over Adlestrop.
A cough and then the engine hissing
Suggested there was something missing

From this gentle reminiscing
    Over Adlestrop.

Willowherb and willows weeping
Breathed like an infant gently sleeping,
With meadowsweet serenely keeping
Watch on hay from recent reaping,
    Round quiet Adlestrop;
The trees composed an arbour shady
Where no bold knight would meet his lady
But an unseen blackbird made his
    Song for Adlestrop

For out from an adjacent thicket
Burst a note so strong and quick it
Startled, though you could not pick it
Out on branch or garden picket
    Fencing Adlestrop;
And in a bright responsive choir
The birds from all of Oxfordshire
And all the birds of Gloucestershire
Sang as if they would never tire
    Round tuneful Adlestrop.

ROBERT BROWNING (1812-1889)
ADLESTROPHE FROM ABROAD

I

Oh to be in Adlestrop now that June is there
For whoever stops at Adlestrop, although quite unaware
That the timetable in all it planned
Had not foreseen this sudden stand,
Hears the blackbird sing on the willow bough
In Adlestrop – now!

II

And after stopping, the engine hisses
And a cough that shows how peaceful this is!
Hark, where the willow herb and meadow grass
Border the field where stooks are piled from mowing
And clouds mirror the hay as in a glass –
That's the blackbird, whose music's overflowing,
Into the throats of Gloucester birds, who capture
Its first fine careless rapture
And pass it on to Oxford birds to sing
In circles echoed in a misty ring –
Plain-plumaged birds but still with song sublime –
No gaudy feathers of this foreign clime.

WILLIAM McGONAGALL (1825-1902)

Yes, you are right that I have a curious recollection only
  of the name of Adlestrop
Where the train in which I was travelling made an
  unscheduled stop.
I say I can only remember the name, but it must have been
On the hot afternoon of Wednesday the 24th of June 1914.

Apart from the noise of the steam, and a noise as if
  someone was preparing to speak,
There was absolutely nothing going on, not a squeak
On the whole station – no passengers or commuters –
And all I could see was the name board with
  'ADLESTROP' in big letters.

But I can remember the names of the various types of
  vegetation
And trees which could be seen quite easily from the
  station;
And the farm seemed to have harvested that blue day
And I thought that the little clouds looked just like white
  piles of hay;

And I remember the chirping made by a particular bird
Nearby, and I convinced myself that I also heard
A lot of other birds which were also starting to do it
In the county I was in and in another county next to it.

ALGERNON CHARLES SWINBURNE (1837-1909)

My mem'ries have burnt to an ember
   Of the place where the train had to stop,
So that now I can scarcely remember
   Any thing but the name – Adlestrop.
It was June when the express drew up there,
   Though the timetable said it would not,
But brimful was silence's cup there
   And the sun was surprisingly hot.

I say that I do not recall things
   But I did scribble down a small note
To remind me of one or two small things
   Like the man who was clearing his throat,
Which echoed the train's exhalation
   Of steam; but forgetfulness' wine
Has numbed my recall of the station
   Except for the name on the sign.

The willow and willow-herb spread there
   And the grass that is green for a day,
And the grass that once grew but is dead there
   And stacked up in stooks to make hay.
Overhead in the summertime brightness
   A cluster of clouds in the sky
Like a parody harvest of whiteness
   Lay lovely and lonely and high.

From the blackbird's bright beak burst out singing
    And to answer the song of the bird
Further ripple on ripple of ringing
    Replies to the sound could be heard,
Till it seemed as if all Oxford county
    Which with Gloucestershire took up the strain
Was imbued with the musical bounty
    That drowned and surrounded the train.

THOMAS HARDY (1840-1928)
"The emergence of the train"

I leant upon the carriage door
   When sun was oven hot;
The train had stopped, when railway lore
   Declared that it would not.
The sign announced it Adlestrop
   And minutes seemed to glide
Like dismal drop on dismal drop
   Of the station's stillicide.

The hiss the engine gave might seem
   As if it cleared its throat
While in the canopy of steam
   I made a useful note.
That up and down and low and high,
   And everywhere between,
All mankind that haunted by
   Were nowhere to be seen

The ancient pulse of willowherb
   The grass and haycocks dry,
Seemed to reflect, but not disturb
   The cloudlets in the sky
And meadowsweet and willow tree –
   Even the humble grass –
Appeared to hint some truth to me,
   But who knows what it was?

At once a voice arose among
    The hedges round about
In sudden unexpected song.
    Blackbird, without a doubt;
And what he sang was echoed by
    The birds of Gloucestershire
And passed on through the summer sky
    By those of Oxfordshire.

So little cause for carolling
    Around the drying crop
Lay written in terrestrial things
    And labelled 'Adlestrop',
That I might think there trembled through
    Those Oxford-Gloucester birds
A secret joy of which they knew
    But couldn't put in words.

GERARD MANLEY HOPKINS (1844-1889)

I caught that noontide nothing but the name
Of Adlestrop, where stopped the non-stop train
At the year's centre, sent my scenting brain
No trace or clue that memory can reclaim.

Engine and man did one thing and the same,
Hissed mist from out their pipes, but how explain
How stationary the station could remain
To lay stress on the sign? For that I came.

Codlins and cream, green grass, and all the willows,
Sweet meadowsweet, hay dry beneath sun's fires,
Clouds echoing stooks below like silk-sack pillows,
Made hush while blackbird's song set off the choirs
That cry their maker forth, from hill to hill, O,
Shout wide to Oxford and its sharing shires.

A. E. HOUSMAN (1859-1936)

In summertime in England
    From east to furthest west
The railways used to keep to times
    The timetable expressed,
    As that was for the best.

Our schedule said we would not stop
    And the mystery increased;
As minute after minute passed
    Since all the motion ceased;
    Ten minutes at the least.

Somebody coughed, the engine hissed
    As engines often do;
The station sign said Adlestrop;
    Though that was nothing new.
    It was the only clue.

The willow and the willowherb
    Grew in the fields around,
And by the grass and haycocks dry
    About the meadow ground
    The meadowsweet were found.

Clouds were another harvest
    To match the one below,
As lonely, white and just as fair
    As balls of gathered snow
    That lads might wish to throw.

That summertime in Adlestrop
    A blackbird sang so clear;
And other birds responded
    From woodlands far and near,
    A happy noise to hear.

Gloucestershire and Oxfordshire
    Took up the blackbird's strain;
Round both the shires they answered
    But though they sang again,
    No movement from the train.

RUDYARD KIPLING (1865-1936)

On a day in June at the height of noon I boarded the
    express train
And it came to a stop at Adlestrop, which Bradshaw
    couldn't explain;
The platforms there were blank and bare, and all that
    transpired was this:
Someone cleared his throat (I made a note), and the
    engine blew steam with a hiss.
The grass and the trees made a rural frieze and beneath
    the hot sun's beam
Of a glorious day, the willow-herb lay, that some call
    codlins and cream.
The piles of hay in their usual way stood out in the fields
    to dry,
As lonely and fine as the clouds that line the wide
    expanse of the sky
Then a blackbird sang and an echo rang in the voice
    from a thousand bills
That caught like a fire through Gloucestershire and
    Oxford's rolling hills.
So this is the lay of the fine June day when I rode on the
    Worcester train
And what's left behind stays in my mind in a way that I
    can't explain.

Masefield confided to Brooke that he was very pleased he hadn't taken his shirt off for this picture.

ERNEST DOWSON (1867-1901)

Last June, yes, late last June, beneath a summer sun
On the Oxford-Worcester line I took the midday express
Which made a halt at Adlestrop, as it should not have done,
And I noted it in my field book, as has become my passion.
    Though there are details I can only guess,
Yes I do remember Adlestrop in my fashion.

The steam made a hissing sound and someone cleared his
        throat,
But no single person left and not a person came;
No real activity of which I might make a note
But I did note in my field book, as has become my passion,
    The empty platform; and, struck by the name,
Yes I do remember Adlestrop in my fashion.

The willows, willow-herb, the grass and meadowsweet
Grew on the banks, and haycocks in the fields to dry
Were still and lonely and fair and every bit as sweet
(As I noted in my field book, as has become my passion)
    As the crop of white clouds hung high in the sky –
Yes I do remember Adlestrop in my fashion.

I have forgot much, it is true, but recall a wider throng
Of echoes and reverberations of a legion
Of birds whose calls, set off by the nearby blackbird's song
(As I noted in my field book, as has become my passion),
    Filled Gloucestershire and all the Oxford region.
Yes I do remember Adlestrop in my fashion.

ROBERT FROST (1874-1963)

What place that was I think I know.
We weren't supposed to stop there though,
No-one to see; nothing to hear.
It's Adlestrop, the signposts show.

The engine seemed to think it queer
And hissed to find no people here;
Someone coughed – his throat was dry
For June was very hot that year.

Willow and willowherb grew close by;
The farms had put the hay to dry;
Above the fields and just as still
The clouds were lovely, white, and high.

The only sound was from the bill
Of a blackbird, and his golden trill
Was echoed through the Oxford hills
And echoed in the Gloucester hills.

JOHN MASEFIELD (1878-1967)

Express train from London, coming to the station,
Pausing in the sun for an unscheduled stop
With a cargo of passengers, one of them a poet,
Who one day will remember this is Adlestrop.

Hissing of the engine is all that breaks the silence;
No-one boards the train and not a soul gets off
To see the view of meadowsweet, willow-tree, willow
    herb,
Grass and hay and clouds, or hear the ghostly cough.

Mourning-suited blackbird, calling in the hedgerow,
Starts a chain of singing on this bright June day
Which is carried by the birds of Oxford, Gloucester,
Somerset, Worcestershire and far away.

A. A. MILNE (1882-1956)

I
Asked myself but
I couldn't
Really answer:
Was there any
Reason why
The engine had to stop?
I
Don't remember if
I gave myself an answer but
The notice
On the station
Said
Adlestrop.
There was
No-one on the platform and
No-one in the waiting-room,
No-one to be seen
Except
I heard
Somebody cough;
Everywhere was empty
And the silence only broken
When the train decided
Suddenly to
Let
Steam
Off.

Willow trees and
Willow herb
Were growing there
With meadowsweet
And rows and rows of haycocks
In the sun
To
Dry
And up above
Another row
Of still and lonely cloudlets
That were white and still
And lovely in a
Bright
Blue
Sky.

In that moment of suspension
(And it lasted just a minute)
A blackbird burst out singing
From a tree
Close by
And all the birds in Gloucestershire
Instantly and mistily
And all the birds in Oxfordshire
Mistily and distantly
Joyfully responded to
The blackbird's cry.

RUPERT BROOKE (1887-1915)
THE OLD STATION, ADLESTROP

Café des Westens, Berlin, June 1914

Just now at the full height of noon
The air with all the flowers of June
Is perfumed, and the summer flowers
Illuminate the languid hours,
And fields take on a flush of gold.
Here railways run as they are told
But there the express train can stop,
Though not as planned, at Adlestrop,
Making again, by no-one's fault,
An English unofficial halt,
When engine with a hiss of steam
Mists empty platforms like a dream
While, as the puff of steam goes off,
Rings dim some disembodied cough.
There willow-shaded meadowsweet
Caresses coolly the bare feet
That run to bathe and, naked-toed,
Step gladly in the Evenlode.

Oh damn! I know it, and I know
The hayfields make a golden show.
Here am I while a bloody war
Threatens to burst upon our shore,
While there things in the summer sun
Go on as they have always done.

God! I will pack and take a train
And go to Adlestrop again!
For that is the one place I know
Where willowherb can freely grow,
And there are cloudlets white and high
Like haycocks in a bright blue sky.

Ah me! does the express still stop
At Adlestrop, at Adlestrop?
And do the willows weeping stand
All unconsoled about the land?
And blackbird with his sombre hue
Sing out as he was wont to do?
And do the other birds take wing
And unrehearsed begin to sing,
For Gloucester birds are sweet of throat
And keen to match the blackbird's note,
And Oxford birds will never tire
To equal those of Gloucestershire.
Say, is that Peace still to be found
And Mystery still spread around?
Still stands the station clock at noon?
And birds sing as they did in June?

e e cummings (1894-1962)

in hot

  mid
   JU   NE
the

trainIwastravellingin
made a sud.
        den.
. S . T . O . P .

Hrrrmph   said cough
SHHHHHH   said engine
but
world had already shushed
and there was
   no-one
       there
           where?
sign   said ADLESTROP

world was still
and full
of willow
   willowherb
   meadowsweet
   grass
   hay
   haystack cloud
and in that still

42

a sud.
    den
blackbird said

SONG

and flicked a switch so
  all the birds
   of oxford ⎫
    &   ⎬ shire
   gloucester ⎭

turned ON

WENDY COPE (1945-   )

Blackbirds are like bloody buses;
Your train just comes to a stop –
For no good reason that I can see –
At I think it was 'Adlestrop'.

You hear the engine making a hissing noise,
Some chap has a cough,
You're trying to see who's on the platform
But no-one gets on or gets off;

And you look at the flowers and fields around,
You look up at the clouds in the sky
And all you can see is the signpost
And that's not telling you why.

But you hear this blackbird, and it's starting to sing,
Just listen, you'll stand there and gaze
While millions of other birds start to join in –
The linnets, the owls, the jays.

A CHILDREN'S AUTHOR

When Theo went to Adlestrop
    Aboard the noon express
It stopped, but why it chose to stop
    The lad could only guess.

The platform, bare as bare could be,
    Had an abandoned air
Which made it plain for all to see
    That nobody was there.

He saw that no-one thereabout
    Wished to get on or off
Though from the engine steam hissed out
    And someone gave a cough.

He noticed one thing straight away –
    A signpost in the sun;
'Adlestrop' it seemed to say
    But that was hardly fun.

But underneath a willow tree
    The flowers grew in crowds,
And up above them white and free
    And lovely were the clouds.

The summer day was warm and rich
    But its attendant hush
Was broken by a blackbird which
    Was singing in a bush

And all the birds that lived around
    Under the Gloucester skies
Joined Oxford's birds in offering
    Their jubilant replies.

So Theo thought it all worthwhile
    For him to make the stop
Because the birds had made him smile
    In sunny Adlestrop.

A MODERN POET

Poet
Place
Train
Stop

Cough
Hiss
Adle-
Strop

Trees
Flowers
Clouds
Crop

Tweet
Tweets
Non
Stop

THE GUEST CARRIAGE

KOBAYASHI ISSA (1763-1828)

The heat. The train stops.
Adlestrop? Somebody coughs.
Birds burst out singing.

Alistair Elliott

.

ARTHUR HUGH CLOUGH (1819-1861)

Say not the poet for nought entraineth
  With thoughts half-hoped for memory's gain,
For though today contentment reigneth
  Tomorrow's traps may unleash pain.

And if 'twere so he could recapture
  Things disparate sensed 'neath fleecy skies,
Green willows, meadows, verdant rapture,
  Pale meadowsweet and haycocks dry;

Or, through the windows, thwart the station,
  Just Adlestrop, a single word,
An engine hiss, a crepitation,
  But yonder, hark, a tuning bird;

And lo! Through mist and heat receding
  A glory of self-kindling choirs
Spreads joy, though of the poet unheeding,
  O'er Oxford's first, then Gloucester's shires.

Allen Bage

MARRIOTT EDGAR (1880-1951)

It were June in the year the war started,
On a hot summer's day I recall,
On a train going from Oxford to Worcester,
And nothing much happened at all.

The train were proceeding sedately
When it came to a halt, unannounced,
But no one got off at this station;
It were 'Adlestrop' – or so it's pronounced.

The platforms were silent and empty,
A bit like the *Marie Celeste*.
And then t'engine gave a loud steamy hissing,
And somewhere a cough cleared a chest.

Around us were scenes all bucolic:
Willows, herbs and wild floral display,
Fields mown and scattered with haycocks,
Drying out in the heat of the day.

Above all this rural perfection
Was the shimmering blue of the sky,
With the sun up high in the heavens
And little white stooks sailing by.

Once again, t'silence were broken
By the song of a single blackbird,
Which was joined by an avian chorus,
Which over two counties was heard

Stuart Roberts

MARY TOURTEL, (1874-1948), ALFRED BESTALL (1892-1986), et al
RUPERT AND THE ADLESTROP EXPRESS

Some while ago, one day in June,
An English summer's afternoon,
I found myself conveyed by rail
Through speeding meadows, hill and vale,

When suddenly our progress slowed
And looking out I saw a road
Which served a quite unscheduled stop,
A minor halt called Adlestrop.

Contrasting with the travel sound
The sudden silence was profound;
A throat being cleared, a hiss of steam
Sole interruptions it would seem

Of a delightful, peaceful state
And what concern if we were late?
I could indeed have sat for hours
Such was the glory of the flowers,

The sight and scent of new mown grass
Not seen by those who quickly pass
And over all a deep blue sky
With dots of cloud far up on high.

Then suddenly a blackbird sang
And distantly a chorus rang
From Oxford, Gloucester and their shires
Sweet singing sound of avian choirs.

Allen Dawes

FEDERICO GARCIA LORCA (1898-1936)
from the Spanish

Yes, I recall Adlestrop.

Her name, a burning afternoon,
Fire-wheel bull of iron, had arrived,
Through the forge of my dream.

Yes, I remember Adlestrop.

Unheralded dark angel visits dying June,
Steam screams from resting black wings,
At a still, naked station.

Yes, I remember Adlestrop.

And willow trees, their wives and their children
Embrace sweet sun warmed flowers.
Summer, loved lonely fiesta, danced
With tiny clouds, on heaven blue sky.

Yes, I recall Adlestrop.

Then, filling my last gifted moment,
A dark song bird sang.
Mist, living with me this life, grew,
In the distance, and through the distance
Flamenco feathered gypsies of Oxfordshire
And Gloucestershire, wept their music.

Yes, I recall Adlestrop.

William McCumiskey